The "I"s in M

Written by
Christine H. Huynh, M.D.

Illustrated by
Darya Obraztsova

Dharma Wisdom, LLC

The "I"s in Me
Bringing the Buddha's Teachings into Practice series
Copyright © 2021 by Dharma Wisdom, LLC

Dharma Wisdom, LLC
Arlington, Texas
www.DharmaWisdomDW.com
books@DharmaWisdomDW.com

Author: Christine H. Huynh, M.D.
Illustrator: Darya Obraztsova

Library of Congress
Control Number: 2021909410

ISBN: 978-1-951175-13-9

First Edition 2021

"I" is an important letter and word for me. It is what I use to call myself. It develops an ego in me – to think that I am the most important of all. My pride and fixed views both contribute to my ego.

The "I" in me is my ego and identity. It makes me feel real and everlasting. However, the Buddha points out that the "I" in me stands for something else – *Interbeing*, *Interdependence*, and *Impermanence*.

Interbeing
Interdependent
Impermanent

These big words that start with the letter "I" are as big as my ego, but what do they have to do with me? I should look into this as the Buddha always has words of wisdom for me to see.

Interbeing means that I exist among people, animals, and objects. The prefix inter- means "between." The word being means "existence." The "I" in interbeing reminds me that I cannot exist alone or by myself.

I come from my mother and father. I rely on my family, friends, and even strangers in order to survive. My parents provide a warm house for me to live in. My friends help to pull me up when I fall down. The food that I eat, the clothes and shoes that I wear, and the bicycle that I ride are all made by people other than myself. Whether they are strangers or people who I know, they are important to my life.

The farmer grows the fruits and vegetables for me to eat. The tailor sews clothes for me to wear. The trucker ships the food to the grocery store for my parents to buy. The community has individuals and groups of people, each with a job that makes my life complete. They are in me and I am in them. We are oneness and are interbeing.

The second "I" begins in the word *interdependence*. It indicates that I depend on other things to be alive. I am made up of the four elements of the universe: earth, water, air, and fire. Hmm ... my true nature actually consists of non-self elements!

My hair, teeth, muscles and bones are made from the resources of the earth. My body grows big and tall, thanks to the fruits and vegetables grown from the ground. Also, let's not forget the milk that comes from the plants and cows.

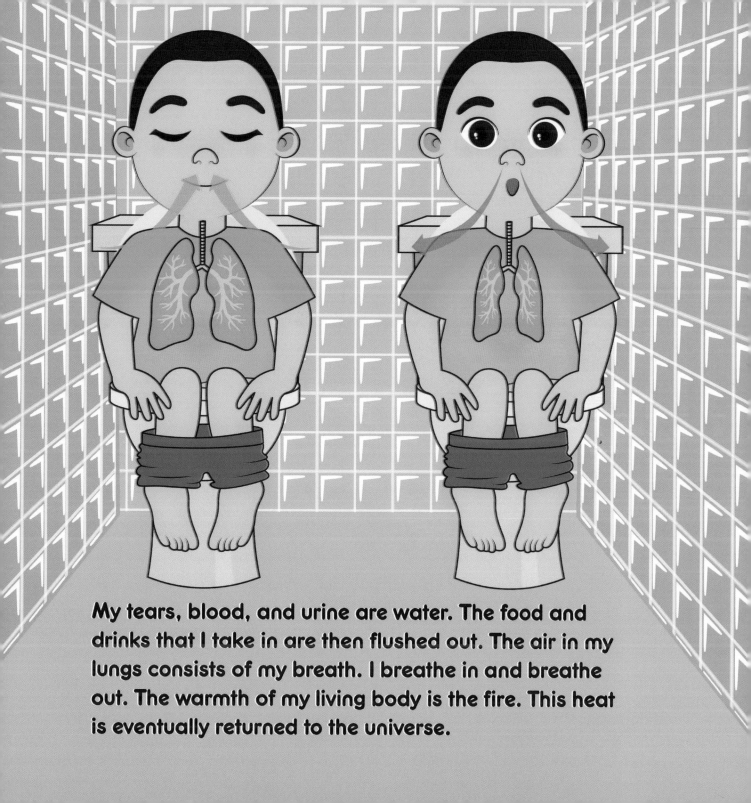

My tears, blood, and urine are water. The food and drinks that I take in are then flushed out. The air in my lungs consists of my breath. I breathe in and breathe out. The warmth of my living body is the fire. This heat is eventually returned to the universe.

Everything that I use for my body I eventually give back to the universe. My presence is dependent on the earth, water, air, and fire of this world. I am "empty" without them. No wonder the Buddha teaches that the "I" in me is not real but is the combination of many other things.

I am interdependent and am one with the entire universe. That means I should protect and care for the environment and everything around me. If the earth provides pure fruits, vegetables and clean water, then the "I" in me is healthy. If I litter and dirty the land, rivers, and oceans, the "I" in me becomes sick.

Interdependence applies to other objects and events in the universe as well. All things rely on one another to exist. As I practice looking deeply, I see that everything is interconnected.

The house that I live in requires a lot of materials to build. It is made up of shingles on the roof, windows and bricks for the frame, and wood and nails to hold it up. Don't forget the carpenter who constructs the house by putting all these parts together.

From this reflection, I understand that a red rose cannot exist by itself either; its true nature is made up of non-rose elements. The beauty of the rose is from the sunshine, water, and nutrients in the soil. Without sunlight and water, it will wilt and return to the ground to nourish another rose.

I see objects and events come and go, depending on the right causes and conditions. The sunshine and water allow the rose to appear, and their absence makes it disappear. It seems like there is a beginning and an end, but it is only the right causes and conditions that transform the objects from one state to the next.

The third "I" is in the word *impermanence*. Impermanence means to constantly change. This is hard to imagine because I feel so lasting, young, and strong. It makes objects and events seem short-lived – like a dream, a fake object, a bubble, a blinking light, a shadow, and dew on the leaves.

My mind and feelings also change frequently. After much
thought, impermanence is just an ordinary process that brings
a positive or negative change, depending on my view.

Change allows me to grow up so I can have privileges such as driving a car or going off to college. However, my parents complain that change makes them grow old and develop gray hair. I am grateful for change because I can feel better and be well after an illness. Or when I feel sad or angry, I can comfort myself knowing that it too will pass.

Certain changes are so small that I am not aware of them, such as the lifecycle of my red blood cells. Other changes can be seen in several days or months, like when a flower blooms or my hair grows longer.

Small changes occurring over time can result in a big change. This happens when my game controller button breaks from wear and tear with repeated use. Sometimes changes can be seen immediately. I may experience such a change when my phone stops working after being dropped on the floor.

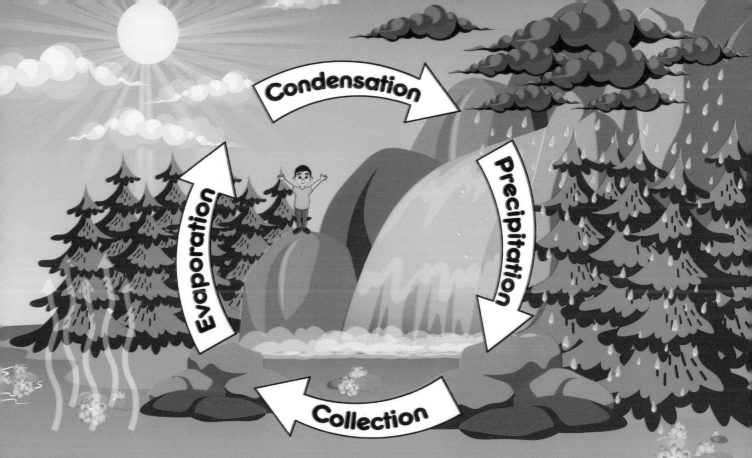

Whether good or bad, changes take place because all the right causes and conditions combine for objects to appear or fade away by the transformation of their form. An example is how water cycles through the different phases of liquid, gas, and solid. On a dry and hot day, water from the lake evaporates into the air, similar to how boiling water turns into steam. Once there is enough moisture in the air, water droplets collect to form clouds. When clouds get heavy with enough water droplets, water in the form of rain or snow is then returned to the lake.

There is no birth or end of the water or clouds, just a change in their form. One thing comes into being in the present moment while the other thing ceases to be present. Life is a cycle with constant continuation.

To live is to have movement or else the absence of life results in a stand-still. The "I" in me has to flow with the changes in time, like a moving river or the life cycle of the water and clouds. Change is unstoppable. It propels me forward to new ideas and a new me!

If I am constantly changing, then who is the real me? My baby pictures show me in a different form than what I am today. I have grown taller and stronger. My feelings and way of thinking are also different with the changes in time.

My body has five sense organs for me to feel and be aware of changes around me: eyes for seeing, ears for hearing, nose for smelling, tongue for tasting, and body for touching. I can definitely do more activities now compared to when I was a baby! I like to swim, ride a bike, and run with my friends. My mind is aware of these new thoughts and sensations to experience all the new changes in me.

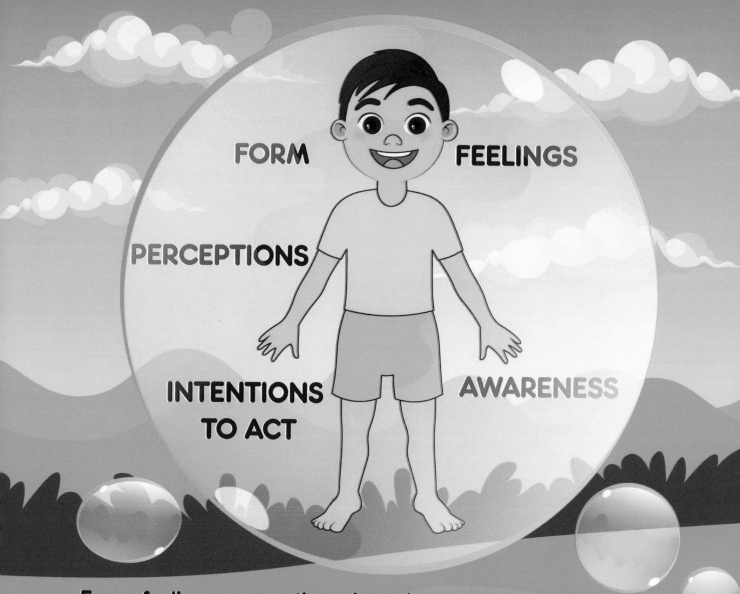

FORM   FEELINGS

PERCEPTIONS

INTENTIONS   AWARENESS
TO ACT

Form, feelings, perceptions, intentions to act, and awareness (consciousness) are called the Five Aggregates. The Buddha states that they give me the experience of my identity, the "I" in me. "Aggregate" is translated from the Sanskrit word skandha, which means to combine and contain as a whole.

My form, feelings, perceptions, intentions to act, and awareness that form my ego and identity change each second. They only exist in the present moment, in the here and now. I must capture and appreciate each experience as the skandhas change and roll into the next present moment.

Who would have guessed that the "I" in me has so many meanings. I am *interbeing* as I exist with other people, animals, and objects. I am *interdependent* as I depend on many things in the universe to live. I am *impermanent* because I am continually changing with my Five Aggregates – my form, feelings, perceptions, intentions to act, and awareness.

Everything in the universe changes and is uncertain. What I can depend on is that impermanence is permanent. Understanding this will prevent any surprises when I experience a change. I can prepare to embrace the events, reflect and look inward, and determine how to adjust to the changes in life. I can practice not clinging to my old form, feelings, perceptions, intentions to act and awareness, as I develop new ones.

Acknowledging these three "I"s helps me to accept my true nature. This awareness allows me to skillfully adapt instead of being weighed down by the changes and attached to the past. It teaches me to have gratitude for the people and all things in the universe. It makes me grounded and realize the "I"s in me.

Printed in Great Britain
by Amazon

24481141R00021